Praise for
Behind the Beard

Santa Buckbee is the best! He is the true personification of the spirit of giving and kindness and love. Enjoy reading his stories of fun and kindness. There is still magic on the earth!

—Dr. William Petit
President, Petit Family Foundation
Connecticut State Representative

Bill Buckbee quite literally embodies the spirit of the season. His love of all things Christmas shines through on every page.

—Lori Capriglione, mother of 4
(including one who believed until the age of 14!)

After reading *Behind the Beard*, I can honestly say that time travel does exist. It brings you back to childhood when things were so much simpler. It reminds you of the memories you had and helps you create new memories with your family.

—Christian A. Carroccio, father of 2

A book written from the heart that inspires readers to reflect and explore their own hearts. The stories shared about a special season touched me deeply and stirred within me my inner child, reaffirming the beautiful magic that exists at Christmas time, regardless of your age.

—Deborah Rose, journalist and mother of 2

Behind the Beard is a wonderful book. Every parent should read it as it gives you insight into how to make Christmas even more special for your children! Everyone has a Santa inside of them. Thanks for reminding us of that, Bill Buckbee.

—Cathy Rehaag, mother of 3

As someone who has photographed a lot of Santas, Bill Buckbee has a most magical way of expressing the true spirit of Santa, which is enjoyed by both children and adults alike.

**—Nicole Bourgeois Believe
Picture This Photography**

Behind the Beard is an amazing book that brings back so many wonderful memories of my childhood. Not only does it bring back memories, but it also sparks the old-time Christmas spirit, bringing out the child in your heart who still lives.

—Tricia Peburn, mother of 3

BEHIND THE

BEARD

Secrets and Tips from The Big Guy
to Help Parents Ensure Belief!

BEHIND THE

BEARD

BILL BUCKBEE

EMERALD LAKE
BOOKS

Sherman, Connecticut

Books published by Emerald Lake Books may be ordered through your favorite booksellers or by visiting emeraldlakebooks.com.

ISBN: 978-1-945847-32-5 (paperback)
          978-1-945847-33-2 (ebook)

Library of Congress Control Number: 2020911205

This book is dedicated
to all the children of the world,
especially those stuck in the body of a grown-up.
May the true spirit of Christmas
reside within, and radiate from, each of you.

Contents

Foreword

Do I believe in Santa Claus? You betcha, I do.
Well, maybe not in the same way that a child does.
I don't believe there's an 800-year-old giant elf who
somehow redefines the laws of physics, space and time
once a year. I mean, imagine sliding up and down mil-
lions of chimneys in a single night while keeping a beard
white as snow!

But I still believe in Santa—his ability to inspire; the
pure joy he brings; how he grants everyone, no matter
their age, the opportunity to dream with the innocence
of a child whenever he arrives. I've seen it year after year,
without fail. Santa is real.

And I'm an elf! But we'll get to that later.

I met Santa for the first time back in 2002. I didn't
know he was truly St. Nick at the time. His peers called
him "Mo," and he was working as a cook in a restaurant.
Not very Santa-like, I'm sure, although his spin on the
house gorgonzola fondue could only be described as
magical. He was a boisterous, fun-loving guy who was

always the life of the party. He was also quite the joker, enjoying both verbal and practical jokes. Have you ever been put into a garbage can by Santa Claus? I have! Mo was fun. There's no other way to put it.

It took me a couple years to even learn that his name wasn't Mo. It was Billy. But, hey! Who am I to question Santa?

We quickly went from acquaintances to very close friends. He was, and still is, a number of years older than I am. We didn't let that stop what would become a very meaningful and special friendship that lasts to this day.

As time moved on, I found myself living in distant corners of the country, but the friendship never faded. He would visit me and I'd see him when I returned home. Over the years, slowly, but surely, Billy began to show his Claus.

There was always something a little different about him. After all, it's not every day your softball team has a left-handed pitcher on the mound. But it went beyond that and his exuberant nature. It occurred to me one day that he was beginning to "look" like Santa. He had been known to grow out his mustache at times, and it was always very light in color. Once he even sported a look I can only describe as a "larger-than-life Hulk Hogan."

Then came the suit. He would, in fact, pretend to be Santa. I say "pretend" because that's how my naïve mind perceived it at first, when I noticed he started to "act" like Santa. Yet even without the suit, he maintained that demeanor, especially around the Christmas season.

The boisterous man I knew didn't exist during the holidays. My friend was authentically a kinder, more charitable and gentler man. This transformation is common for many during the holidays, but I quickly realized it went well beyond that for Billy. He even traveled once all the way to Mississippi to spread some joy to southern kids one season. That's going above and beyond for the cause!

Eventually, it clicked. I was able to see past the suit into his heart and soul. I came to the astonishing conclusion that he was indeed Santa Claus. It might sound silly to you that some guy I randomly met in a kitchen and played poker and softball with would turn out to be Kris Kringle, but hear me out.

No, he doesn't live at the North Pole.

No, he doesn't fly around the world delivering gifts at a pace that defies the laws of physics. Nor does he own a reindeer, let alone nine.

But this man has proven to me time and again that he truly is the human manifestation of the spirit of Christmas. Nothing means more to him, especially around Christmas, than bringing love and joy to everyone he comes across, from stranger to best friend, from child to senior citizen. The amount of happiness I've seen him bring to people over the years is incalculable. It's an uncanny gift that could only be possessed by the true Santa Claus.

I eventually moved home and was reunited with my friend, who had changed drastically since we first met—and all for the better. Older and wiser of course and even a little bigger, naturally... This is Santa we're talking about after all! But there was also this new quality of selflessness that I didn't recall from before.

That first winter home began with a night where everything changed for me. I went to a community tree-lighting event that advertised Santa Claus himself would be there! Surely, I couldn't miss such an opportunity to meet the real Santa. Upon his arrival, I thought something looked awfully familiar about St. Nick... The way he talked, the way he looked. To my surprise, even behind a stunning beard as white as snow, I realized who it was.

So I watched as this master of ceremonies lit the trees in the center of town to a rousing ovation by its citizens. Then every single family, one by one, went up to meet him and take a photo with the *real* Santa Claus. I was quite a distance away, admiring this from afar, hearing his "ho, ho, ho" ring out from time to time. The happiness of everyone filled the crisp New England winter air.

I wanted to go say "hi" to my friend before leaving, but the line never seemed to get any shorter, and I wasn't about to cut in front of a bunch of kids who had been waiting patiently in the cold for their turn to climb onto Santa's lap and wish for whatever it was they hoped to find under the tree Christmas morning.

But that night changed my perception. I saw Billy truly as Santa Claus.

Shortly thereafter, he brought me up to speed on the duty he has to keep the Christmas spirit alive for everyone he sees. He told me how he can give any Scrooge or Grinch a pure heart with the innocence of a child.

Christmastime is a magical time of the year. People are nicer and more charitable. But it all starts with Santa Claus, and he takes that responsibility very seriously.

Okay, so back to that thing I mentioned about me being an elf...

No, I'm not one-foot tall.

No, I don't make toys.

No, I don't have pointed ears... unless you count the prosthetics in my closet.

I became Santa's "Chief Elf" to help him spread his joy to countless others. I told him to let me handle the logistics and I would create a well-oiled sled... er, machine... so he could focus on what he does best—bringing joy into the lives of so many people. I even helped him expand a single Christmas Eve visit into an entire night's worth of visits, which have been some of the most magical moments in people's lives. I mean, what would you do if you were a kid and found Santa under the tree delivering presents at 2am on Christmas morning? That's a priceless gift that I was happy to help him bring to so many.

At the end of the day, Billy doesn't just look like Santa—he doesn't just put on a suit and parade around. He truly cares about everyone and is obligated to make every single person he meets as happy as possible.

Santa Claus isn't a once-a-year thing. The beard goes strong year 'round to the point where kids approach him in the middle of June and ask him if he's Santa. Without skipping a beat, he gives them a wink and a nod. Similarly, the kids who have seen me elf-ing with Santa have been known, on rare occasion, to call me out. I have to hide my ears to recite one of the several lines that we have for such an occasion. The kids know when they see him, even mid-summer, that they just spoke with Santa. It keeps them smiling, reminds them to stay nice, and brings a little of that Christmas magic back, even if only for a moment.

I'm not going to get into why Santa does what he does. That's for him to explain to you in this book. But know that it comes naturally and authentically. Most importantly, it comes at his own expense. It's not easy to be the most important man, or elf, in the entire world. All of his free time, and I do mean literally every single second, goes into making others happy, even at his own expense. He gets completely run down each year because every hour of every day he's out there with the same energy, spreading love and Christmas cheer.

Trust me, when the beard is white as snow, those eyes can appear as red as Rudolph's nose! So it's my job to make sure he's taken care of because it's his job to take care of every other man, woman and child. It's an honor and a privilege for us both, but also a unique obligation with a level of importance unmatched by almost any other role in the world.

And that is no easy feat because not everybody is happy during the holidays. He's had children sit on his lap as their parents were half a world away at war. He's visited families who lost a child the week of Christmas. He's been able to absorb the sadness of others in order to bring them a glimmer of hope or happiness when they need it most. And that's the true spirit of what it means to be Santa Claus.

And what I've seen makes me believe.

Peace, love and happiness to you all, and have a very Merry Christmas.

—Myke Furhman, aka "Butters the Elf"

Preface

THIS BOOK IS NOT INTENDED for the eyes of children. It is written for parents and grandparents, uncles, aunts and great-grandparents... It's made for family. It's the "Teacher's Edition" to Christmas, in a way. This is not an Associate's Degree for the holiday, but a simple tool to help make it a little better. This book is intended for those who believe and want to keep the magical, classic concept alive a bit longer in a world of technology and skepticism.

The wide-eyed optimism of youth fades far too quickly, and if we can work together to preserve that, to extend that belief for just a short time, then we have allowed that one childhood to be a bit happier.

We have allowed the magic of Christmas an opportunity to survive.

I was raised to believe in Santa Claus, and I still do. There was a time in my teens when, sadly, I lost that belief. It was an awful time in retrospect. But my belief completely returned when I put on that red suit and saw myself through the eyes of children.

Santa is quite real. You simply need to know where he is and how to help deliver what he represents.

You are an elf. It's great to be an elf. Elves get to keep secrets. At times, you will be Santa too and, as long as you know when to be the right charac- ter, you're a step  ahead. This book is full of secrets, and it's your duty—nay, your obligation—to preserve, execute and create great memories, and to pass along the traditions of our youth.

If you disagree with believing in Santa Claus, then stop here. You're too far gone, and I won't have it. On second thought... Stick around, I may just win you back.

In this book, I will share with you some tips to help your entire family, from eldest to youngest, make their belief even stronger. I will also share stories that have touched my heart or brought me to tears and those that made me laugh uncontrollably from my hundreds, maybe thousands, of appearances as The Big Guy. It is a story that reassures you that the spirits of Christmas and Santa Claus are both alive and quite well. I hope to show you how I see it, to help you look at it differently. If you get the privilege to see for a moment what I have seen, then you'll "get it." It is a true pleasure for me to share my experiences with you.

Chapter 1 – Being and Becoming

IN A SMALL NEW ENGLAND town in the 1970s, a teacher informed our third-grade class that we would be performing a play for the entire school. Everyone would be there, and it would be our first chance to act on stage. At that age, there was no larger audience that you could possibly imagine.

The play was to be an adaptation of the great American poem, "'Twas the Night Before Christmas." One boy stood up, reaching as if trying to touch the ceiling tiles, and shouted, "Billy should be Santa. He has the belly already!" While kids can be cruel, it was never taken as such (I wasn't even *that* portly of a boy), and I was excited to be considered for the part. This particular role would grab hold of me for a lifetime.

My classmates were dressed as reindeer. Nine kids with paper antlers were strung to me with twine. We had cut out their antlers with those blunt-nosed scissors we used in grade school (that cut absolutely nothing).

Moreover, can I add that I'm a lefty and those "left-handed scissors" never worked at all?

Anyway... My sleigh was made of bright red cardboard accented with black and tons of glitter for that special *wow* factor. There were no amazing special effects, and our performance was held in the cafeteria of the school, still reeking of yesterday's canned green beans and sloppy joes. The beard was scratchy, the suit was too big, and I tripped over the rolled cuffs while trying to hold up a sleigh that was missing suspenders, but fit like clown pants.

It sounds like a wreck, but it was one of the coolest things I've ever done to this day. I found that I loved the spotlight and that day its fluorescent glow released my inner ham.

A classic figure in history can be played by any mediocre actor and often is. Historical or fictional characters are usually quite well-defined and only require a basic understanding of the individual; then you apply your own personal adaptation. To play Abe Lincoln, for example, you throw on the beard and top hat and you look the part. Recite the Gettysburg Address and you're off to the races. You've succeeded and will be somewhat believable.

To capture a historical figure like Daniel Day-Lewis did in the movie *Lincoln* requires a gift and a talent. It demands that you believe you are that character—that you *are* Abe—and your performance must be infused with that belief to be great at what you do. I've never spoken to the aforementioned Academy Award winner, but I believe he channeled a bit of the former president while preparing and shooting, whether he knows it or not.

My adaptation of Santa Claus is no different. It's just a role I reprise and adapt to annually. So yes, odd as it seems, I take "being Santa" as a serious thespian undertaking. I owe it to the children of the world to live up to the expectations our parents have presented to us and exceed them. The question I constantly challenge myself with is, "How do I be Santa... *better*?" You are Santa as much as I am, or at least you can be. You need to work at it too.

I am strictly the physical representation because, quite simply, I look like the guy. If I looked like Tom Selleck, I'd be doing Magnum PI spots for... Well, no one does spots for that show anymore. But you get my point. I was born with the rugged good looks of Burl Ives, Edmund Gwenn and Ed Asner. So be it. I accept it and run with it. I look like The Big Guy so I work toward perfecting the part.

At forty-eight, I am currently one of the youngest professional Santas in the country. When I first started getting paid to do this, I wore the fake scratchy beard and plastic shoe tops.

Eventually, I grew my beard and added make-up so it would appear more real. While it looked quite cartoony, it was better than before. Then, I grew my beard every year in anticipation of the season, dedicating five months to the process. Now, I keep the beard throughout the year since I run the risk of being recognized at the grocery store in the summer months.

A natural beard is key to the role. Kids spot a phony a mile away. It's hard work not shaving, but I'm getting pretty good at it. I bleach out whatever isn't already grey, although each year I need less bleach. Santa also has an excellent Brazilian-American stylist named Sergio who works on his beard. I hope that doesn't make me a diva, but I've been called worse. Sergio is excellent at what he does, and I couldn't be a great Santa without his efforts.

This Santa is also bald. This is not strictly a Santa choice, but I do prefer the clean, polished look of a bald Santa. I also have no problem removing my hat and allowing children to see Santa without it. Many of my favorite old cartoons show Santa as bald, and those were always what I've based my look on. Does it really matter? Absolutely not! I am glad my baldness can go to some use, though.

I have multiple Santa suits in my collection these days, but to give you an idea of how they differ, I'll describe a few here.

I have a traditional suit of plush fur that I call "Fuzzy." It's just that, and I feel like a stuffed animal when I wear it. It's very warm so the mid-December outdoor appearances are far more comfortable.

I have a flat-finish suit that photographs better, but isn't as warm. That one I call "Scratchy" because it is, and I have to wear something underneath to keep it from touching my skin. It allows me a cleaning rotation as well.

Finally, I have the suit I call "Miracle." It is inspired by the movie *Miracle on 34th Street*. Miracle is a men's red suit with two-tone shoes, a gold vest, and a bowler hat. It's quite classy. This suit draws more attention than the other two combined.

I go the extra mile of re-investing in my suits each year to keep them up-to-date, ensuring they are photo--worthy, and to make sure each one still fits. Santa's "Cookie Zone" does tend to expand a bit each year. The suit is not just an identifier for the public. It's an energy given to me when I see it in the mirror.

Finally, I don't wear white gloves unless I'm wearing Miracle. I believe that Santa prefers black or brown leather gloves, or even mittens. White gloves are for the bush leagues. When you go pro, you become a bit more conscious of the details. I get asked about my gloves all the time. The black gloves I wear match my black belt perfectly, and besides, who wouldn't wear leather when they're holding the reins to a sleigh?

Quick Story

A little girl bounced across the room and launched herself onto my lap. As she landed, she exclaimed, "Santa, I pooted!"

I couldn't help but laugh. Her mother was glowing with embarrassment and said, "She knows people laugh when she says that, but she didn't fart on you, I hope!"

Even if she had, it could be worse!

Why one elf is crying I'm not sure.
It looks like quite the party though!

Chapter 2 – Power of the Suit

I CAN ONLY RELATE IT TO the '70s TV show *Greatest American Hero*, where this regular guy named Ralph finds a suit filled with power. He doesn't quite know how to use it, but it helps him find inner strength he otherwise never would have known. Ralph spent his life trying to figure out, tweak and utilize the powers it possessed. I don't know if he ever got to completely understand it since the show was canceled, but I've always wondered.

The Santa suit has great power and, yes, Stan Lee, with great power, comes great responsibility. We must be kind, but not syrupy sweet. Santa has a rough side and is allowed to be a *little* gruff at times, but *never, ever* mean. I must *always* be willing to say only those things I would say in front of my mother or niece. A swearing Santa is not one I recognize as true to form. The same goes for a drinking Santa. Santa should never smell like Grandpa's garage. There should never be a whiff of booze, smoke or any other substance, save that of a cookie or cocoa.

Let's briefly discuss the smoking part. Santa traditionally has a pipe. This is certainly acceptable and a wonderful accessory to the costume. It makes for a nice image of Santa at home by his fireplace enjoying a pipe. But I don't recall ever seeing him smoke in front of children—so for me, it's a "no go" in public forums.

Pure joy radiates from that suit when worn properly, which I've not experienced anywhere else in my life. The energy I feel when wearing the red suit and assuming the role is like no other. I know that at some point during the day, someone will lose their grasp on reality, child or adult, and for that small sliver of time... They Believe. I have seen the look in the eyes of grown men who, for a second, stare with awe because they were suspended for just that one brief moment outside of their preconceived reality.

What they are experiencing is far more than a fat guy in a suit. They believe in the joy of the holiday. I grant them permission to remember and believe in the pure joy of youth. There is good in mankind. Belief can be restored when I put on the suit. It's that simple at times.

Quick Story

Sometimes a sad home life can rear its head in the most unlikely or unwelcome places, like when visiting Santa. A little boy climbed up onto my lap very quietly one day and just looked at me.

His mother, standing behind him, said, "Jack, tell Santa what you want."

Little Jack hugged me and said, "I want Santa to be my Dad."

Mom looked at me and shrugged with a very sad look and waved her hand as if to say his father had left them.

What can you say to Jack? "Santa loves you very much, Jack. I don't think Mrs. Claus would let me move, but you can write to me *any* time you want, and I will write back I promise!"

Jack smiled and nodded, while Mom, with a tear, mouthed, "Thank you."

Dear, Santa   you are sweet. I am
thankful for you. How are your elf's ? Tell
them I'm thankful for them to. Thank you for
every toy you have gave me for christmas.
Tell your elf thank you for making all the toy's
for good little boy's + girl's.
Tell Mrs. Clause I love Her. And I love you to Sant
a. i wont a Mp3 player and a pupie and I wont
Bud Back not a new one. Tell your elf's I love
them to. And help your self at anything
food anything and help your self at ~~any~~
the candy canes. It has ben my dream to
go to the north pole. and

Happy Holiday's.

Chapter 3 – Where Do You Start?

YOU ARE A NEW PARENT or maybe one who simply wants to make the experience stronger for your child. Extraordinary! The fact that you're reading this book shows you *do* care about creating the most magical experience possible. It's always work. It has to be, so make no mistake. I can't provide all the answers, but the fact that you're looking to make it better speaks volumes that you *do* bother. You *do* want to make it different and special and, most of all, memorable.

I don't care what your job is. I don't care how much money you make. Your child's Santa experience will always have its foundation in how well you know them. This is not a book on parenting, but it's a book on providing the best possible Christmas experience for a child. To do that, you need to know as *much* about them as you possibly can. *You* make their Christmas experience special, not the presents. That perfect gift does help, no question, but *that* comes from knowing the child very well.

Preparation doesn't mean just buying the right present. It's about knowing your child well enough to know what they'll really enjoy and how to make that gift into a special experience for them.

Yes, you need to know what they truly like and what might *wow* them. But knowing your child will give you the best information on what toy they will especially enjoy and which one won't end up getting thrown out with the wrapping paper.

So, don't get caught up in the fact that it may seem like all they care about is the newest video game or which trading cards Santa left them. It is the experience that lingers, not the toy.

Don't become the parent who sits with an open flyer for the local toy store and tell the child to circle what they'd like. Are you kidding? I'd circle half the flyer! Then a commercial comes on for the newest stuffed creation that you can sleep with, teach to dance and swim, do your homework on its belly, and jam toys in its mouth while it makes fresh brownies giggling, "I love you." Now your child *has* to have that.

No! That's not the point here.

Choosing a toy is certainly age-specific too. The one- or two-year-old doesn't usually grasp the concept of the holiday, but that three-year-old? Look out. They're getting it. By the time they're four, they have this holiday thing down. They know what they want, and they get really excited.

This is a fun time to watch as they develop a sense of awe. By the time they hit six, some begin to question, but this is very workable. Allow them to ask and respond with magic and awe-inspiring visuals of the North Pole. If you can get a child to believe until eight, you've done your job and anything after that will be borrowed time and should be considered bonus rounds.

Regardless of how long they believe, it's your job to make each Christmas memorable for you and for them. Take pictures on Christmas Day. Don't forget to do this. It's easy to get wrapped up in the flying paper and hopefully the laughter, but what do you want to remember or record for years later? How do you want them to remember this Christmas when they're thirty and getting their kid's presents wrapped? If you prepare, you can make Christmas a strong part of a wonderful childhood.

Quick Story

A little girl got on my lap and, when asked what she wanted for Christmas, she said, "A choo-choo and some chicken!"

Try to feed your children before visiting Santa.

An example of what I see sometimes and,
in my opinion, what not to do with a child.

Chapter 4 – It's Gotta Be Memorable

REMEMBER YOUR FAVORITE CHRISTMASES AS a child. Do you remember the toys specifically? Sure. Some of them. I remember getting Star Wars figures and being so excited. I can't tell you what year I was given Greedo or the Hoth version of Luke Skywalker or my X-Wing fighter, but I can certainly tell you that I opened them in the living room, sitting on the couch, and that I jumped up pumping my fist because, whether I knew it or not, it was exactly what I wanted!

I also remember my first bike. Santa had left a note that there was something in the garage that he couldn't fit under the tree. I followed a string out to the garage to see a shiny, new, red bike with a white banana seat. I remember more that my grandfather got on my new bike and was riding it in the driveway while it was still dark out in the morning. I have a picture of him laughing that will never leave my mind. The gift itself was nowhere near as special as the memory it created.

My grandfather and that bike are both long gone. I busted those handlebars over many jumps. We'd fix it and do it again. It was a good present. Clearly, it was one of the best ever. The memory of that first morning, how I got that bike and who I shared it with, will live with me forever. Why? Because my parents took the time to make it memorable for me.

How do you make it memorable? Great question. Imagine there is a pile of presents, all wrapped perfectly. Your child tears through them on the gravity-defying mission of getting wrapping paper to hover in the air while seeing the gift as the paper lands. They are overwhelmed with joy and excitement and can't wait to open the next gift. It's likely that you feel they didn't even appreciate the one they just opened, especially if it's clothes—the vegetables of the Christmas present feast.

How do you make one present memorable? If you can't afford a mountain of gifts or if you choose not to overindulge and only have three gifts, how do you make them special?

First of all, you need to slow down the process on Christmas morning. I suggest having the whole family watch one person as they open each gift. Children will emulate how parents receive their gifts. So, show some excitement and appreciation when Dad receives another packet of underwear. Junior needs to see Dad open his gift and see that reaction before the next gift is passed.

This is one suggestion. It's entirely on you to decide if you want to do it. You know your child and what they respond to, and what makes them smile. Family traditions can inspire great memories and, like a great vacation, a basic outline needs to be planned.

Quick Story

"Santa, I want a puppy." Well, this is a request I get a lot that requires a look to Mom and Dad who nod (or not). They did neither.

I said, "Hmm... We'll see. Have you been good?"

He replied, "I sure have Santa, but both of my other puppies died this year, so I need a new one."

How about some fish?

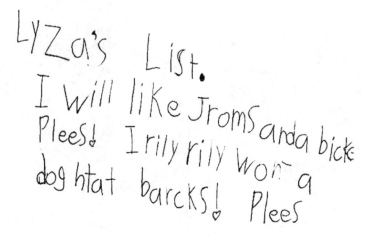

I believe this translates to:

Lyza's list.
I will like drums and a bike.
Please! I really, really want a
dog that barks! Please.

I love it.

Chapter 5 – Family Traditions

I DON'T REMEMBER EVERY TOY I received every year. I *do* remember waking up all excited and following my family's traditions on Christmas morning. The first rule was: you had to stay in your room until Mom and Dad came to get you. Mom, to this day, is the biggest kid and can't sleep on Christmas morning. She is up at 4:30am, ready to go!

Know what your family traditions are and ensure that they're upheld, and feel free to add a few new ones of your own. Your best friend may have one hidden gift for the kids to find or make sure your family has breakfast before opening any gifts. Small things like this are still a strong piece of my childhood, like having sausage and eggs before I could open my first present.

Since my teenage sister was always the last one still asleep, I was allowed to go jump on her bed to wake her up *that day only*. Now *that* was a great tradition. Part of our morning meant the smell of Dad burning the Jimmy Dean breakfast sausage patties in the kitchen and grumbling about the burner being too hot. I can still taste it because everything tastes better on Christmas morning. The aroma of Jimmy Dean is as Christmas to me as the smell of pine or holly.

We had to wait at the top of the stairs until all of the kids were ready to come down. We could see presents under the light of the tree, lit from above. It was amazing to see. The glow was like a fuzzy dream state when I think back on it now. In front of us on the stairs were our stockings, all stuffed and looking at us, begging to be rifled through, but those had to wait until after the other gifts were opened. In each one, there was surely candy and oddly some fruit. The fear of coal made us nervous with the stockings, and we usually got some to keep us honest. No one is good *all* year, right? Each of us had a homemade stocking that Mom had knit and would fix when it got a hole. Dad didn't have one. For some reason, he had a shoe. I still don't know why, but it was funny that Santa filled his shoe.

A fun tradition we have always enjoyed, and still do, was the wrapping paper disposal. When we finished opening a present, we would roll the wrapping paper into a ball and throw it into the trash bag. Of course, this bag always sat next to Dad, so he was pelted with a lot of wrapping paper balls. I don't think he could have enjoyed that more. He still expects it to this day.

He gets back at the kids (and grandkids now) every year when he wraps one present over and over with packing tape, duct tape and anything else he can think of. He binds that thing tight. It takes him weeks to complete his "work of art," and you never know who will get it that year. The recipient is usually my older brother, but sometimes me. Inside (once you get there) is a trinket.

A keychain. A band-aid. Something trivial. Mom, always with her camera in hand to capture the moment, can never stop laughing.

Establish those individual family traditions. These will be far more memorable than the actual presents they receive. Santa isn't anywhere near as important as your goofy family traditions. In our house, Santa wrote different names on each gift, like "That basketball kid" or "Fozzie Bear's biggest fan," and Mom would read these names off. I certainly was Fozzie's biggest fan too. I loved my bowties. Wocka Wocka! Each of us would be excited and have to stop and think for a second or two, then suddenly blurt out, "Wait! That's me!"

Santa often gave me replacement socks addressed to the "basketball guy," so I knew he was thinking about my amazing hoop skills and wanted me to look good in my knee-high socks.

Quick Story

I had twin boys on my lap. They were roughly five-years-old and were both dressed alike. One was certainly a ring leader in the making as he had control of the entire visit. He went first with his list of new games and trucks. When he was done, he leaned over to his brother and under my whiskers whispered, "Tell Santa to bring me presents!"

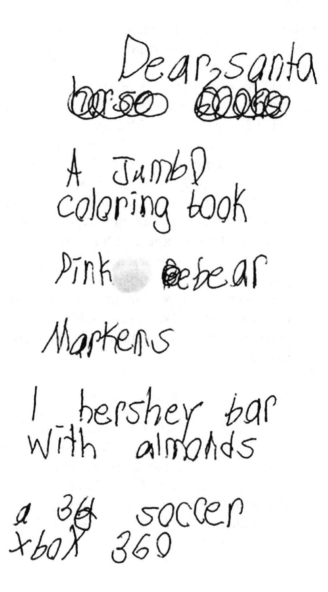

Dear santa

A Jumbo coloring book

Pink bear

Markers

1 hershey bar with almonds

a 3d soccer xbox 360

Okay, I'll get the candy bar.
Mom and Dad can get the rest for ya, buddy!

Chapter 6 – Santa Starts at Home

SANTA IS A GREAT JOLLY old elf, right? Not always. Let's be frank on this topic. Just like Mom and Dad, Santa is clearly judgmental. That's not a bad thing to preach at home. While Santa delivers presents to the good boys and girls, he also delivers coal to the naughty ones.

Kids need to be good in order to get presents and candy on Christmas Day. You can certainly utilize Santa's awe and power to invoke good behavior or encourage them to clean their room, but know that once they are face-to-face with Santa, they will be a little scared of this powerful guy who judges them throughout the year. So, allow Santa to make the child smile too. Don't over-do it.

Be sure to reinforce the good behavior at home to entice the motivated child into being happy about seeing Santa. You need to ensure it's a healthy fear of Santa's power, like a child has for a parent. To know Santa can say "no" just as easily as he can bring gifts is of vital Christmas importance. The relationship with Santa is cause for respect, but he needs to still remain very likable. It's of significant value to prepare this for weeks or even months before your visit with Santa. Fear of the wrath of Santa will not result in smiling photos, nor will the child enjoy the experience. It may also get Santa peed on, and we'd like to avoid that at all costs. If you prepare them with the encouragement that they are good kids and Santa weighs the good with the bad, then the child has far better odds of getting the gifts they desire.

Appreciation for what we all have is tough to discuss with a child who may have never gone without, especially around the holidays. Concepts of charity and giving need to be taught, or at least demonstrated, at a young age. I have heard many sad stories of a child simply asking for a jacket or mittens while sitting on Santa's lap.

A great lesson in compassion is to allow your children to "be Santa" and experience the gift of giving to those less fortunate. Let them pick out a couple of toys or a jacket or sweater for a child who wouldn't otherwise receive those gifts. Tell them, "This year, we'd like to help some kids who don't have as much as we do, and we want Santa to be able to bring them some things. Wouldn't it be nice if we could help Santa?" Include this act in your letter to Santa as an effort to teach a child how to give back. This lesson teaches the great joy of giving and helps them begin to want to help others, a trait which I sadly see as fleeting these days.

Quick Story

A little boy climbed up on my lap and stared with wide-eyed wonder. I said, "Hello, there... Have we been good this year?"

When he opened his mouth to speak and the corners of his mouth turned down, he said, "Santa, I scared!!" He cried and froze, the poor little guy.

I can be scary, but I certainly never intended it. Sorry, buddy!

Dear Santa,

May I please have a,

Finger nail thing,

Long slinky,

Barbie video,

Laptop any color,

An elf that is not an elf on the shelf

And a phone that can do anything except for call. ☺
Thank you Santa!

Love,
Kieredith

Chapter 7 – Letter to Santa

THE CLASSIC TRADITION OF WRITING a letter to Santa is great practice for helping the child focus on what they want and actually ask for what they truly desire. It also allows parents to understand what the child is dreaming of. It doesn't matter if the child can write yet or not. Write it for them until they can, but *always* write the letter.

This should be done with some cookies and milk (yes, my personal favorite) or hot cocoa. Usually, for me, this was done at the kitchen table. This should not be written wherever homework is done as it's not to be confused with work. They should be excited to write their letter to Santa and share how good they have been.

The letter shouldn't be just a wish list of toys. It should list things they've done to *be* good. This allows the child to think about what else they could or should do to help out and be better. "I cleaned my room this week and helped Dad with the dishes, Santa. I like to help around the house, and I hope you saw me. I also did my homework and asked questions in class." Allowing the child to quantify their efforts and qualify their requests is a nice life lesson, no?

I highly recommend writing the letter around Thanksgiving weekend. Some prefer the week before because Black Friday is upon us with great bargains. Unless your child needs the hottest TV or there is another Furby out there that has a small window of availability, don't trip over Black Friday. Some people gasp when I say this, and I know it is a tradition to kick off the holiday for some, but that is one tradition I steer clear of, regardless! And please don't go shopping on Thanksgiving. This should be a holiday for all, and the staff at the mall has to come in? That's just not right in my eyes.

If you want my best advice, go to the mall on Black Friday after 6pm. This is the time that Santa himself shops since all of the kiddies are home eating left-over stuffing and pie. They can have the pie. I want the cookies. It's a well-kept secret that I share with you now after many years of utilizing this time as Santa's secret shopping time. The way I see it, you've bought the book so we are friends now. I share with my friends. Come shop with me when the malls are empty. The shelves are re-stocked, the place echoes with my footsteps, and the deals are usually still running. I find it the quietest time to shop in the entire holiday season.

You can actually hear the mall music, and the staff is fresh and willing to help. Okay, enough about the mall...

Writing the letter early allows you time to send it and get a response. It is also time to get that tree up after turkey, so why not kick off a Christmas tradition that weekend? You can certainly mail back a response yourself or go online as there are a number of places that will send a personalized letter back from Santa. His response should be encouraging of their good behavior and should mention that it looks like they're on the Nice list. Yet Santa stating that he can see that they aren't brushing their teeth can be pretty motivating.

Quick Story

A blind child was placed in my lap and asked, "Santa, is it really you?"

"Why, yes! It is." I answered.

He tugged the beard and said, "Yup, this is the real one, Mom!" A good beard tug never really hurts, so go ahead and let them.

Chapter 8 – One More Year

I LOVE MY PARENTS AND LOVED my grandparents when they were still with us. If you're a great parent with a desire to keep the dream alive, you can certainly extend your child's belief.

I was twelve when I stopped believing, temporarily. Twelve. That's right, folks, I was a believer for a very long time as a child. I was hoodwinked by my parents and grandparents, and they carried it off quite well. Of course, at the time, I felt a little foolish since my friends all stopped believing at eight or ten, but looking back I appreciate their efforts even more.

My best memory was in my last year believing as a child.

Getting wise to their tricks and listening to my friends who no longer believed in Santa, I could thwart their efforts and call them out on their game. Like a G-man, I would keep my parents covered and totally secure for the entire night. I would sleep just inside their bedroom doorway (behind the door that opened *into* the bedroom) thereby using my body as a blockade to their leaving the bedroom without my knowing about it. *Ha! This will put an end to their ruse*, I thought! Smart kid. Not quite smart enough to know I am as sound a sleeper as you could ever find. I sleep like a rock. They waited until I passed out and Dad just slid me over. Off they went.

In the morning I awoke, face against the door in my sleeping bag, knowing that, "Ha! They didn't get out, so it can't be them!" Low and behold, a mountain of presents awaited me, and ole Santa pulled it off entirely. What an amazing guy!

Another fun "extending the holiday" story was when I was taking requests one day and staring at the line of children who were waiting. Santa can get a bit concerned that it will be "more of the same." I look for something to entertain me as well. A dad snuck behind the scene to share a story with one of my elves, who came to me and whispered a little trickery. It would seem that his two boys (ages eleven and twelve), named Brett and Brad, were on seriously borrowed time in belief, and they were in line with their mother to see me. On the ride over, they were preparing in the car to call me out. They were saying, "There is no Santa and, if there is, he won't be *here*. Let's ask him what we got last year. Aside from Mom and Dad, no one else could know." Smart kids. This might have stumped me somewhat.

I have a rule as Santa that I explain to the children. I always portray that I am Santa, not some helper. If you don't think I'm real or challenge that I am *the* real Santa, then you risk coal or, even worse, you could receive reindeer poop in your stocking. This is only if I can show you that I am indeed the real Santa.

By the way, reindeer poop is put in a sandwich baggie and oddly resembles small chocolate candy. The North Pole is chock full of that stuff. I have more of that than snow even. Dasher is a poop machine—but I digress.

So, the story is shared, and the dad gave us the info that last year they'd received a mini-bike, but they don't take care of it. It is sitting in the corner of the garage just gathering dust. Dad disappeared so the boys wouldn't see him, and I awaited their appearance in line. They stepped up and my elf gave me a nod letting me know these were my unsuspecting victims of Santa magic. They stood in front of me, arms crossed as if ready to confront a bully.

I greeted them with, "Hello, boys. I'm Santa."

They scowled, looked at each other and, the older one, Brett, said, "Are you the *real* Santa?"

"Well, of course, I am! Who else would I be?"

The boys looked at each other and Brad, with this youthful arrogance, asked, "Oh yeah? If you're the real Santa, what did we get last year for Christmas?"

"Well, boys... You do know that if you question the *real* Santa and you're wrong, you certainly run the risk of receiving coal or, worse yet, a pile of reindeer poop. It's not nice to question Santa. Are you sure you want to ask me that?"

They looked at each other and smirked, and Brad said, "Yup. What did we get?"

I replied, "Well, boys. That mini-bike was difficult for my elves to complete, and I'd hoped you'd take better care of it. It just sits in the garage gathering dust these days. It makes me a bit sad really. But Brad, Brett (their jaws were on the floor at this point with their eyes as wide open as possible), maybe you could go home and help Dad clean out the garage today and get it running again. Now, where would you like the reindeer poop dropped off? I do have so very much of it."

The boys apologized profusely and jumped to Santa's lap grinning ear-to-ear for their photo. Dad was in tears laughing about thirty feet behind the camera. Mom thanked me, and Dad waved. That, to me, is one of the great perks of the job.

Quick Story

On a very busy day, a little girl was placed on my lap. It is not uncommon for parents to just drop them there. She had the prettiest little dimples and was so happy to see Santa. Mom and Dad were taking pictures, and the little girl had a nice visit. I got her a coloring book and, as I went to put her down, her mother stopped me. The child was missing a leg.

Santa paused, and the little girl never skipped a beat, saying, "It's okay, Santa. It's okay to be different, right?"

It sure is, my dear. It sure is. Santa needs to pay more attention though!

My Pipi Says
Hi and she
wants Candy

I really don't know how to respond to this.
It speaks volumes by itself.

Chapter 9 – Pick Your Santa

Santa Claus isn't just a prop for a photo. Visiting Santa should always be an experience. It is something to plan for and build up to. The day you get to go see the man should be exciting and thrilling, like in A *Christmas Story*. It should never end with a kick down the slide, though, and if you're not careful in choosing your Santa, that can happen, so to speak.

Research your Santa. Try to find a local photographer who works with Santa and plan that visit. You may spend a little bit more, but you're not getting a value meal at the fast-food place. Spend the extra $20 or $30 to give your child a memorable experience.

Many small towns and communities do a breakfast or lunch with Santa. These are usually far smaller settings and that Santa is there typically as a volunteer. Yeah, he may have the fake beard, but he likely has the right heart for the job. Talk to him. Ask for a little individual treatment for your child. The more information you can feed a good Santa, the more they can sneak it in there for the kids!

Here are a few tips to make the actual visit better:

- Be sure to say your child's name as they are going to see Santa so he can use it.

- If you have an Elf on the Shelf (and I highly recommend you do), then be sure to mention their name in front of Santa. A good Santa will run with that, so use the elf's name.

- Mention to Santa that report cards just came back great, and ask if he got the report from Mrs. Smith (or whoever the teacher is). He can use that information as if he's spoken with the teacher.

- If you have a dog, be sure Santa knows their name. Kids *love* when Santa knows a good dog and will bring it a treat.

- Find out if Santa will be visiting again anywhere else. Another visit with the same Santa can reinforce concepts and ideas.

- If the child needs to work on something, bring it up. "If your bedroom were cleaner, you would have room for more toys," Santa might say to persuade the child to tidy up their toys.

- Finally, enjoy the experience. Have fun. If you're relaxed and having fun, your child will as well. If you're tense, they're tense.

Quick Story

A little girl, about ten-years-old, sat upon my lap. She was clearly on the cusp of disbelief. Her grandmother was with her and had a sour look upon her face.

Grandma said, "You tell him what you want."

"Yes, ma'am," she softly replied. The little girl asked me for a pink coat. A very easy request, but a very sad girl.

I asked, "Is everything okay?" She nodded.

Her grandmother returned and pulled her off my lap by her wrist and said, "Well, did you ask him?"

The girl looking at the floor responded, "No, ma'am."

Grandma looked me straight in the eye and snapped, "You'd better not have. Santa can't bring Daddy back!"

I still pray for that little girl.

*Santa, on bended knee, is taking a moment
to remember the true meaning of the holiday season.*

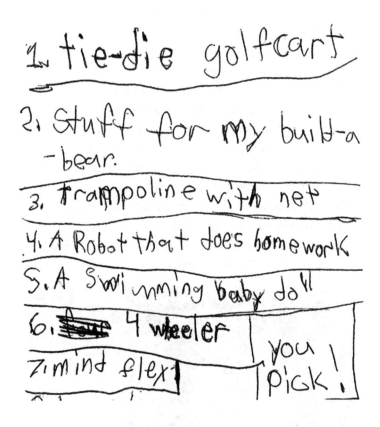

1. tie-die golfcart

2. Stuff for my built-a
-bear.

3. trampoline with net

4. A Robot that does homework

5. A Swimming baby doll

6. ~~four~~ 4 wheeler

7. mind flext

you pick!

Not only can Santa pick,
but numbers four and seven are both challenges!

Chapter 10 – Mall Santa

I HAVE PLAYED THE PART IN multiple states and, yes, I've even been a mall Santa. Although you'll never convince me again that it's a good idea, I am glad to have done it.

I have enjoyed the memories that I luckily kept in a journal, which was sent to me by a friend. That blank journal came with a note that said, "Write down your stories." I have. You're reading them here. One of the best gifts that Christmas was a simple, yet thoughtful, care package sent from friends back home. Santa appreciates a gift, and moreover, some good friends.

For reasons I'm about to share, the guys who accept the role of mall Santa every year are saints in my eyes. You wouldn't believe the conditions they work under! But many of them get the opportunity to work with their wives, who manage the camera, which is wonderful.

They are usually very nice people, likely retired, and making some good money for the holidays.

I am not a proponent of mall Santa visits. These guys receive minimal breaks and are on the clock for all of those extended mall hours. I worked those hours as a younger man, and I was *wiped out*. Fifteen-hour days, seven days a week, is a lot for anyone. But when you're likely over seventy and that line of moms is screaming at you to hurry up, it takes its toll and the Santa magic fades.

Santa's staff is seasonal help, so they're usually people looking to make a few extra bucks for their families for the holidays. They sign up for the job because working with Santa sounds really fun.

Sometimes it is. But most times, it is screaming and crying kids in the midst of a meltdown due to long lines and long-expired patience. Other times, it's a parent fighting over the charges and photo packages, which the staff has zero control over.

I was lucky to work with a wonderful staff in the mall that year. They were genuine, friendly people who cared about this visiting Santa, put up in a crappy motel and knowing no one within five hundred miles.

What many people don't know is that the mall Santa is hired (usually) by one of two companies that provide the talent in every mall in the USA. So, while you may feel great that you're supporting a retiree and their spouse, the majority of the money goes to a large organization. Not that big corporations are bad, but it likely is not what you think it is. The money does not go to a Mom-and-Pop organization.

Now, the one I worked for was financially sound and paid generously. The demands of the hours, however, did not make this the happiest of environments.

Santa's breakroom is usually an unused storage room, and the best ones are already taken because it's the biggest holiday of the year. I was so incredibly tired after just the first week, and you can't call in sick, you can't take a half-day off. You're the only hope for those kids to see Santa!

I called my office one day on a break and found that they had a "roving Santa" who might come by to provide a day off. But he never came. Instead, he had to cover a four-state territory because one Santa broke his hip and two others had pneumonia.

What am I saying?

Look at your mall Santa when you walk by. Is he smiling? Is he interactive? Is he just a part of the scenery, or is he providing a true experience for the children? If it's a conveyor belt with cookie-cutter snapshots, you may want to aim your sights a little higher. Mall Santa is usually a great guy, just seriously overworked in my humble opinion.

If you *do* visit a mall Santa, I recommend these tips:

- **Plan your visit.** Many people will wait until the last minute, so go early in the season and early in the day. Morning Santa is *far* happier. After school, it gets crazy, and after work, even more so. The less time you spend in line, the lower the odds of that meltdown.

- **Have compassion.** Those people helping Santa are not making much and have dealt with angry parents and screaming kids all day. Your kindness goes a long way.

- **Lower your expectations.** Expect the least amount of happiness and be thrilled if it's more. Accept it when it isn't.

- **Do not expect to share letters and stories.** Instead, plan for your kid to get their first

DMV-type photo experience. Sometimes they place the camera trigger on Santa's lap and, when your child's butt hits it, the photo is taken. Perhaps a slight exaggeration, but you get my point.

One last thing about the mall... That year when I was far from home, someone broke into my vehicle and stole my GPS. I certainly needed it to get back home. My connection was very strong with friends around the country via social media. I shared my stories and escapades, some of which you've read here. I shared that I'd been robbed and other things were taken too, and it was just disheartening. Not that I'm different from anyone else, but who steals from Santa? It hurts the holiday spirit.

A grade school friend from many years before read the "stolen GPS" post and decided that Santa needed some good cheer as well. I was already, for all intents and purposes, miserable doing the mall job, but this only added to my experience. She decided to lift my spirits and give a gift to Santa. She rallied some anonymous old friends and classmates (some of whom could well have been a reindeer from the third grade), and she collected money to replace my GPS. I told her as generous and touching as this gift was, I couldn't accept it. She made it quite clear to me that this was not an option. People had already given their money and that was that.

The gesture, from someone who I rarely see and who was some 1,300 miles away, was overwhelming to me. I cried. I felt the warmth of the holiday spirit. I did replace the GPS and used that money to do so. I still have it. I still smile when I use it. It's difficult to accept gifts at times, but this one certainly touched my heart, and she will never fully know the impact that gesture made on my life and my Christmas spirit.

Quick Story

"Santa, someone stole my bike. I don't need a brand new one. Can you just get me my old one back?"

Sheriff Claus, on the case! Check your neighbor's house.

Dear Santa,
    Did you know that I want a Paper Jam Guitar and a train with a track. (no Geotrack)
This is the end Santa.
I Love you Santa!
    Love, Aidan.

I'd better get these gifts out quickly because, apparently, this is the end!

Chapter 11 – Recognizing Yourself

I**N ALL MY YEARS OF** being Santa, I've come to recognize that most kids and their parents fall into clearly defined categories when they're around The Big Guy. The variety makes my job very interesting at times...

Let's see if you can recognize your child in any of these descriptions! You decide:

- The Giggler – They cannot stop laughing because they're so happy.

- The Highly Excitable One – This kid is just freaking out so much they don't know what to do!

- The Soft Talker – Santa is usually older, so speak up!

- The Mute – Nothing said, no response. Nothing.

- Santa's Best Friend – Buddies for life! They will have a tough time leaving.

- The Crier – *Many* kids cry, so have fun with it. I do. I make a crying face too! They'll love that picture someday in their high school yearbook, no?

- The Screamer – They freak out when they see Santa and can't stop screaming.

- The Terrified – Maybe 1% of the kids I see are *completely* terrified. Do not force them to see The Big Guy, please.

- The Pee Kid – Everyone talks about this kid, but it's so very rare. Most do not pee on Santa. It's a legend. A story. It's possible, but not the norm.

Just like kids, parents can easily be sorted into many categories. Here are the usual suspects:

- The Fun Parents – The dream. Casual, relaxed and enjoying the day.

- Over-Into the Holiday – Matching sweaters, anyone? For Mom, Dad *and* the kids. Not a bad thing, folks. To each their own.

- Grandma in Charge – Covered elsewhere in this book.

- Grandma in *Total Control* – The aforementioned on steroids.

- Mom Knows Better Than Santa – Correcting The Big Guy makes belief tough to pull off. Let Santa go on a roll unless he calls for help! This mom usually also knows the better camera angle, the better way to wear Santa's hat, and the better cocoa. Santa can't win here.

- Tough-Guy Dad – Too cool for Santa? This Santa will target that like a bee to a summer soda can! Have fun. It's for the kid.

- Make 'Em Cry – These parents know the kid will cry, but can handle the moment of tears for a lifetime of smiles in that picture. I respect these parents. They actually get it and the photos are far funnier!

If you recognize your child (or yourself) among these descriptions, don't worry. Santa loves you anyway! But this would be so much more fun for all of us if you'd let our time together unfold naturally. I've got this!

Quick Story

I have had children (more than one, which is sad) climb onto my lap only to tell me, "Santa, I get everything I ask for, so I hope you're ready!"

Certainly, the spoiled mouths of youth do not know what is appropriate. Of course not! They're spoiled.

One child asked me for a boat and a whale. I'm not sure they get the concept here.

Chapter 12 – Talking to Santa

I AM A SANTA WHO SPENDS his time with each child. I do not enjoy the conveyor-belt Santa experience. I like to talk to the child and let them have a few moments with The Big Guy. They've waited a whole year to tell Santa how good they've been. This is why my lines were crazy long in my mall days, but I didn't care. The mall did, though. They wanted volume, and I understand that's what they're paying for, but to me, the *experience* is paramount to being Santa. Kids want time with Santa, and they deserve it.

When you're seeing a Santa who can take a little time, bring your letter in person. Santa can slip it back for posterity, but let him read it in front of them. Let him see the picture your child drew on it. Include the letter in the photograph too! Why not?

Maybe equally as important, as a parent, allow this to happen naturally. Many parents have ideas and want to be sure their child says what they need the child to say. "I need him to say he wants a fire truck because I already bought it!" This brings me back to knowing your child before you buy gifts. This prompting confuses the kids. Sitting in my giant chair, I see parents do this *all* the time.

The kid is crazy excited. They are sitting with a *hero* of theirs. Allow them a moment or two to take it in and catch their breath. They are likely in awe and now someone is telling them what to say, telling them to ask a question, pushing them to say something. In the time it took you to read that sentence, I have had parents ask four or five questions to their child, and the kid gets so lost. That is not an exaggeration. The best visits will develop. If Santa needs help, he will certainly ask.

Quick Story

Two kids came to visit wearing matching sweatshirts that read, "Santa can't beat Pop-Pop."

This type of shirt is fairly common. And my rehearsed response is, "Santa agrees!"

Santa always speaks well of others, although it's fun to tell Grandpa he remembers when Santa had to give him coal when he was a little boy. It's all in good fun.

On this one day, before I could even say anything, Grandma yells at Santa, and not in a playful way, "Well, *you* only come around once a year, and *you* get all the credit!"

Wow. She was seriously upset that Santa was getting all the glory for the gifts. What can you do but shake your head, smile and wish them all a very Merry Christmas?

Chapter 13 – Grandma and Grandpa

GRANDMA, SANTA LOVES YOU. YOU taught us to be good at constructive criticism, right? I hate to say who the biggest culprits of confusing children are, but it's Grandma. She is usually *at least* as excited as the child, if not more, and she is talking *a lot* and telling the child to look at her for a photo, then to tell Santa what they want. Look over here! Where's your woobie? Who's Grandma's boy? *Stop!*

Remember why you're there. A good Santa will do all of these things for you. He will engage the child in conversation. He will be sure to get a good picture. I am not saying *all* grandmas are like this, but the overwhelming majority of the ones I see are exactly like this.

I had a grandma come see me once with twin boys (about two years old) with their three-year-old brother. Clearly, she had her hands full, so one might expect a comment like, "I've been in line with these guys for an hour. Please help!" She does not ask for help. She has two crying kids and a third running in circles around Santa's chair with sticky popsicle hands, screaming. She's lost all control. Then she starts telling the photographer where to put them and what angle she wants. Put them? No one can even catch them! I am convinced they had pixie sticks and ice cream for lunch because these kids are wired. They have fresh batteries.

Finally, she looks at Santa and barks, "Since you're not helping, we're going!" and she storms off, the kids waving their hands and screaming all the way out.

What did she accomplish? Was anyone enjoying that visit at any time?

It has been my personal experience that this is who should take the kid to see Santa: Grandpa. I have asked every grandpa I've met what he wants for Christmas, and the most popular answer has been a resounding, "I want that child to be happy and have a Merry Christmas" or "To see my kids enjoy themselves." That's it. Some dads do it too, but most dads don't make this trip, which is a statement in and of itself. The grandpas I have seen come to visit Santa usually define "real man," and I'd like to thank them for taking that time. Here's to hoping that rubs off on their children and grandchildren.

Quick Story

A little girl, who I had been seeing every year since she was about three, came to visit me at an event. We were raising money for a local charity. It had been a long day of scheduled visits, keeping me busy since 9am and it was now closing in on 9pm. Her parents always booked at the last minute, so they got stuck with the late visit. They never once complained and were always incredibly patient as we usually ran a little behind with a very personal visit.

This little girl is so sweet, with long blonde hair and wearing her Christmas PJs. She looked like a cartoon character with her big baby blues and huge smile, happy to see me after waiting all day. We had a lovely visit and I was just about spent, but she had a surprise in store for me. After our visit, she ran over to her mom and came back with a gift for me. I was perplexed. No one brings Santa a gift, do they? Cookies and milk were plenty for my needs.

She climbed back into my lap and asked me to open the gift bag. Inside was a Santa hat with a Chicago Cubs logo. This was the year the Cubs had won the World Series. They had seen the hat in a store. Her dad told her that this was Santa's favorite team, as he followed my "secret identity" on Facebook and had seen my recent posts of pure joy and excitement.

She asked him, "Daddy, can we get it for Santa?"

It was one of the greatest gifts *anyone* has ever given me. Each year since, she brings something for Santa, and each time I am surprised, elated and truly touched.

Chapter 14 – Favorite Requests and Questions

SANTA GETS TO KNOW PRETTY quickly each year what the hot new toy will be. I do, on occasion, hear some pretty outrageous requests. Some make me laugh on the spot even though the child is as serious as reindeer poop!

Here are a few of the funny things I've been asked for over the years, in no particular order:

Child: Santa, I want... your hat!

Little girl: I want a pink banana.
Santa: Why not yellow?
Little girl: Because I'm a girl!

Little boy: I want Batman cereal!
Santa: Now?
Little boy: No, for Christmas, Santa!
Easy kid to please.

Little buzz-cut boy: I want a ponytail!

Child: Santa, do you sleep with your elves?
Santa: Why, no. I don't fit in their tiny beds!

Child: Santa, I'm gonna eat the Oreos I was gonna leave out for you. I like them more than you do.
Great... no cookies.

Child: Santa, Mommy wants a boob job.
Mommy was not amused. Her face matched my suit!

Little girl: Santa, I want a pink 4-wheeler and a cupcake.

Little boy: Santa, I want Cheetos and two snails.

Santa: What do you want for Christmas?
A little boy (who had been smiling until fear overtook his face): To get down!

Quick Story

Creative kids make for a fun experience, and these are all great. The one that takes the cake was a 6-year-old boy who asked me for a shotgun. I told him that Santa has issues sometimes carrying firearms across state lines, but he assured me it's all he wanted. I asked what he would shoot with this gun, and he threw his shoulders back and very seriously blurted, "Reindeer."

I said, "Not *my* reindeer?" to which he replied, "Yessir." Well, a polite hunter. I said, "Why would you shoot *my* reindeer?"

He exclaimed, "Santa, they're on my roof… Easy pickins!"

You can't argue logic, I guess. Dad was smiling hard behind him, so proud of his boy. I think Santa should do a pre-flight fly-by at that house.

Chapter 15 – Heart Strings

WHILE IT IS THE MOST rewarding job at times, my suit has certainly seen its share of tears as well. Santa cries. Children with special needs or simply a special request can be the most rewarding visits for Santa.

I have been privileged to spend a day with the family of a little girl who suffered through years of chemotherapy. For her last Christmas, I was requested to pay a home visit. She had a little brother and an older sister. The older sister didn't believe anymore, but she may now.

Santa just walked in with arms full of presents and said, "I heard this family wanted a visit, so I decided to break my own rules about traveling at night and come say 'hi' myself!" I put the presents down and took a knee. The little girl I'd come to visit walked over and gave me a big hug. Santa was certainly choked up then and thinking about it now as I write this brings tears again.

Her mother told me, "I haven't seen her smile like that in months."

That little girl didn't make it to another Christmas, and I hope that the year Santa came to visit helped create some extra-special memories for them all. It's a great gift to be able to give a little bit of joy to a family in need of a smile. That little girl inspires me to this day, and I see her smile clearly all the time. That entire family's experience of the day and their smiles shared with Santa still inspire me.

Quick Story

"Santa, I have all the toys I need... Can you make Daddy happy?"

Santa needed a break after this encounter. A true, and unprompted, giving child, who motivates me even more than most.

Chapter 16 – A Santa Visit

IN 2012, AN ACQUAINTANCE OF mine called me up to ask for help. It would seem a mutual friend, who was a single dad with two little girls, had a less-than-jolly ex-girl-friend who decided to end their relationship just a week before Christmas. They had lived together, so this would be hard enough for his two little girls. He had just moved them out of their school that year (just a couple months before) to a new house in a new town. The girls, who live in Connecticut, had just lost some former classmates in the Sandy Hook tragedy. When the girlfriend left, she not only took the presents for the girls, but even took the tree. Who takes a tree from children at Christmas?

So, we collected a few bucks from some of our acquaintances and a few more came in from elsewhere. Then, I called this friend to let him know we were all rallying around his family. Santa was going to step in on this situation for his girls. He fought with me, not wanting to accept the gifts, but I said, "You can either tell me what the girls really want or you can make me guess." He finally gave in, told me, and on December 23rd, I went shopping for two special little girls who I'd never met before.

Seeing the looks on children's faces when I'm in the grocery store is one thing. I get that a lot. Dressed normally, kids tug on their mother's pant-leg when they see me, saying, "It's Santa!"

When I walked around Toys "R" Us that day with two carts full of toys, kids were on their *best* behavior! Jaws hit the floor all over the place. That always makes me chuckle and, of course, I let out a "Ho, ho, ho" or two to make it even more enjoyable for me. We returned and wrapped the gifts, but I had one more very important job.

On Christmas Eve after bedtime, I went to their house. My friend had invited his ex-wife over to witness this experience. He had bought his own tree and decorated it with the girls. I walked in with bags full of wrapped toys and stuffed the stockings. The look in his eyes was that of a child himself, believing in Santa. This was Christmas magic.

I told him to call for the girls who came out in their PJs to see none other than Santa himself in full red suit, putting their presents under their tree. We enjoyed the milk and cookies together and even took a couple of pictures. Two very happy girls should now believe in Santa until they are thirty, at least.

Chapter 17 – More Home Visits

THAT FIRST VISIT AS **S**ANTA to someone's home left me wanting to offer something truly unique to people. It reminded me that life's greatest memories are made of experiences, not *things*—a memory can be the best gift of all. So, ever since that first home visit, I have opted into the incredibly unique experience of Christmas Eve visits.

It all began quite innocently. A friend who knew nothing about my first home visit reached out and said that their very wealthy employer wanted to do something cool for his five-year-old daughter. I was asked what I might charge to come by their house in the full suit on Christmas Eve.

Now, for me, Christmas Eve had always been my personal family time. The night before Christmas was and is important to my mother. Mom would invite friends and family to come by and spend a little time together. Not that everyone stayed long. They often had someplace else to be on Christmas Eve. But it was always nice to see friends and family pop by and visit.

Some brought gifts, and Mom always bought something extra to have on hand when the unexpected opportunity to reciprocate appeared. Chocolates. Hot coca sets. Just something as a token gesture that would be wrapped and put aside upstairs. She would say "Oh, I am glad you stopped. I have a little something for you too!" Then she would run upstairs and write their name on the tag before delivering it. I'm sure people knew, or maybe they didn't or didn't care. It's that wonderful feeling of giving that just cannot be measured against any other emotion.

So, when I was asked to miss out on the party, it was difficult to say "yes." Then again, a hefty check on Christmas Eve (when I had run myself dry buying gifts for everyone I knew) sounded pretty enticing, so I accepted the invite.

What I never expected that night was that I would find a new calling and passion in visiting this little girl.

I met the dad in their gated community in a building set away from the house. Okay. House might be a bit weak. This was a mansion. A gorgeous home. Dad greeted me with a couple of gifts and some background information about his little girl. He told me her school, her teacher, her pet's name... a tremendous amount of information, to be certain. I promised to retain as much as I could, and he brought me into the house. Yeah, the "house."

Behind the enormous doors, I found a giant room with two fireplaces. The room was more of a ski-lodge bar area; all-natural wood and cathedral ceilings. The fireplaces were set at either end of the room with about forty yards between them, separated by leather couches. Quiet

Christmas music was playing, and the room's dim lighting allowed the fifty-foot Christmas tree to simply glow.

Thank goodness only one fireplace was lit as I would make my appearance from the other. At 6'3" (plus the boots), I wouldn't fit well in most fireplaces, but I could actually stand inside this one... with room to spare. I could see cookies and milk on the table along with her note, backlit by the other fireplace. It truly looked like it was a set for a Hallmark moment—simple and beautiful.

Once Dad had me situated, he went upstairs to get the guest of honor. As I saw the door open from the bedroom on the overlooking walkway (it was *way* up there, but I could make out what was happening), I stepped slowly out of the fireplace with my sack over my shoulder.

I could hear them whispering, but ignored any noise as I had work to do. I went straight for the cookies (don't judge), then directly to the tree. I knelt down and began taking the gifts from the sack. Then, I heard her giggle.

I will never forget that giggle. It was accompanied by goosebumps shooting up both of my arms. I turned to see an enormous smile, showing me that she was likely expecting the Tooth Fairy as well. Exactly as you might imagine, she was missing her two front teeth, but none of her smile.

She ran across the room, which would have had me gasping. (I told you the room was huge.) She leapt into my arms and gave me the biggest hug. As I have said before, the pure joy of a child is truly one that cannot be duplicated. She held onto me with sheer belief and nothing else. Her mom and dad stood back with giant smiles and smart devices extended, enjoying the moment.

What amazed me even more in that moment was that I remembered all of the information that Dad had given me. Her teacher, her dog and her Elf on the Shelf's name all came flooding into my brain like they were my own memories. They all gasped as I told her that I had gotten positive reports from her elf about school and all of her recent activities. Dad tried prompting me to mention other details (which scared me to death), but I worked through it all. After that, we took some photos and shared milk and cookies. We delivered *pure Santa magic*. There is no other way to say it.

She was allowed to open a couple of presents with me, but I told her she needed to go back to bed so I could go get the rest of her presents, and she couldn't watch. If a child is ever going to behave, it's in the presence of St. Nick himself. Another hug and off to bed she scurried.

Dad brought me out through the basement (which was bigger than my apartment at the time—I mean it's crazy how big this place was) and back to my truck. He was grinning like she had been, and I must have appeared to be a mirror image.

I looked at my watch and the entire experience had lasted only 15 minutes. It had felt like an hour to me, easily. Then I realized my hourly rate was almost embarrassing, but Dad was so thrilled he asked me back until she was 10.

Life changed along the way for that family, but that only child became a good friend to Santa. I don't know if she ever stopped believing, but thanks to her, I believed even more strongly.

I had just experienced something completely new to me. It was unlike any other appearance I had made, and I wanted to duplicate it immediately.

On my way home from the mansion, I texted an old friend who has three boys. It was about 10:30 or 11pm.

and I knew they'd be awake putting gifts out. I said "I'm in the suit and about ten minutes from your house. Wanna surprise the boys?"

I think the boys' dad was equally as surprised as he was thrilled and said, "Yes!"

I delivered a similar experience, getting caught under the tree, and these three almost knocked me over. They couldn't believe they had caught Santa, and there is photo evidence that hangs on their wall to this day.

I knew however that I had found a niche in the Christmas market, and it was one I would fill for years to come... with no intention of ever stopping.

On a side note, Mom and Dad slowed down and eventually stopped their Christmas Eve tradition. As wonderful as it was, people get busier and, well, they still pop by on Christmas Eve, but it's not a party anymore. Yet if you swing by their house today, I guarantee she has something wrapped and waiting upstairs for you.

Chapter 18 – Buttery Expansion

YEARS AFTER THE MANSION HOUSE visit, I found myself stopping here and there, but not really expanding the business side of things because it was frankly a lot for one person to do. A few extra dollars at the holidays didn't hurt, though. And it was allowing me to replace some pieces of my suit, plus expand the wardrobe a bit. I didn't know how big I wanted this business to be.

Then, along came Butters... Butters is my CEO (Chief Elf Officer) of the Santa Claus Company (santaclauscompany.com). This was the smartest thing I have done since losing the white gloves. Butters came in as a business partner of sorts, to begin with. His real name is Myke (but he needed an elfish name) and he is one of my dearest friends. Who knew that what Santa really needed was a little Jewish elf?

Butters began handling the business side of things and expanded all that we do. I still maintained all of my complimentary appearances (as every Santa should), but he added business appearances as well. Butters built a website and offered video messages from Santa and FaceTime options. We were taking Santa into the 21st century. Finally!

Butters actually has three Emmy's to his name and is a talented producer, editor and cameraman. This made videos around the world possible, and we have delivered that.

He offered to not only put the Christmas Eve visits on the website, but also to collect data, handle the sales aspects, and even drive the sleigh on the big night.

Over the years, we stepped up the technology. At first, I would study sheets of information for each child. I'd read all about them and then hope I'd remember inside the house. What Butters introduced, though, saved my brain. We bought the smallest Bluetooth device possible, and he would speak with me from the sleigh, reading from the sheets. Brilliant!

This was the smartest possible move until we found ourselves in neighborhoods with poor service. In Connecticut and eastern New York, there are surprisingly many homes with minimal cellular signal. But with every problem comes a solution,

and now we ask for the home's Wi-Fi password to avoid any concerns.

Butters and I have had many quality adventures, but one truly stands out among them. We had a family with a mom and three children. Dad was away in Bahrain and unable to be home for the holidays. The children were ages 11, 6 and 4. Their gifts were left in the garage, and I was to enter through the kitchen. No problem. As this was in our first year working together, there was no Bluetooth for us to use, and I had 5 to 6 pages of info on each child. I was hoping to remember 2 or 3 things about each of them in my 5 minutes of study between stops.

Moving quietly through the kitchen, I could see the TV was still on, with Buddy the Elf singing away quietly. As I turned the corner, I saw two trees. Seriously people? Which one?

I saw one was by a fireplace and noticed my plate of cookies, so I stepped up to get one. Okay... I grabbed two. As I turned around, sack over my shoulder, it really looked like I was stepping out of the chimney. At this moment the 11-year-old was across the room, coming downstairs because she had heard something. Her mother was waking the younger children. She stumbled backward into the doorway, hand covering her mouth. This moment is burned into my mind forever.

I didn't know what you are about to read until after the visit, but let's rewind three hours.

Mom was putting the young ones to bed, and when she walked by our 11-year-old's bedroom, she heard sobbing. When she slowly opened the door, she found her oldest child sitting up in bed, crying in the dark.

Mom shot to the bedside and asked what was wrong, assuming the girl was missing her dad for the holidays.

While she did miss her dad, she had been persuaded by her classmates that Santa wasn't real. She was mourning the loss of her own childhood innocence. We all face a similar moment, or at least those of us with a heart do.

Mom told her that it was up to her whether to believe or not, but to remember that not all kids get visits from Santa. Maybe they were just bad kids. Perhaps that's not the nicest thing to say, but these kids were destroying all that she had worked for. Mom had to understand that, at 11, it may be time for her to stop believing, but she certainly had a secret up her sleeve as all great moms do!

The child told her it was over, but she wouldn't tell her siblings, and then she rolled over to sleep.

Fast forward to the look on that same girl's face when she saw me eating a cookie by her tree and then calling her by name. A lightning bolt of pure joy hit her in that moment. She had completely convinced herself that Santa was not real. She had wept over the loss of belief. Then, just hours later, she is woken up by a noise and finds her entire world flipped upside down.

As had happened to me before, every tidbit of her information filled my head; school stories, congrats on an award she had just won, a local farm where she visited a pig, and I knew the pig's name! *Insane!* While all of this happens, Mom is still upstairs. She comes down to see her daughter beaming and sitting with Santa. Mom can tell it's all back.

Mom gets extra points for not taking a video, but living in the moment. Instead, she took it all in, but she didn't smile. Mom didn't say anything, except when she told the kids to gather with Santa to take a picture for catching me.

I have that photo that Mom took after the other kids came downstairs. It's not one I share with the world. The smile on that 11-year-old's face is proof that Santa is real and likely means she will believe until she's thirty, at least.

When I got back to the sleigh, Butters asked how it went. It's tremendous to have someone there to share these experiences. I was bursting with excitement that it had gone so well. I told him that I was perplexed about Mom though. She didn't smile and seemed almost cold to me, but I hoped she had liked it.

As Butters always does, he texted Mom to ensure she was satisfied with her family visit. It was then when Mom shared the night's experience with the crying child with us. Mom said that she was holding it all in so her daughter would not see her tears of pure happiness that she had booked Santa this one night, this one year. She was only sad that her husband could not be there to experience it all too.

Santa shed a tear for that family that night and does again while writing this. Butters did too. Two guys sitting in a minivan crying. Would have been a great stop for a police officer, no?

This evening still moves me more than I can explain to you. It's a Christmas I will cherish forever, and I thank Butters for that gift. If he hadn't stepped in to make the Santa Claus Company more of a business, I would never have had this unforgettable experience, nor would I have had so many since that night too. (And the growth of our business has allowed me to buy more suits as well as an ever-needed cooling vest for under the suit. It gets hot inside homes when you wear fur!) Thank you, Butters. L'chaim, my friend.

There's a postscript to this story. I was invited back the following year so Dad could experience it when he got home. On this visit, the tears were his.

Chapter 19 – Operation Mistletoe

T HE HOME VISITS WE HAVE made are truly unique and something I am proud to offer. Over the years, they have grown from a "one-off" to a specialty and then into a regular occurrence. It's something I am proud of introducing as I have seen it restore belief and that is what I am all about: establishing and maintaining belief.

Two friends of mine, a married couple who regularly take advantage of my public visits, shared an interesting story that I will do my best to convey here.

Their two children (a boy, 8, and a girl, 6) were discussing Santa one afternoon in December. Both were true believers and had no doubt about the fat guy in the suit, but they were eager for more. They devised a plan. When I say "devised," we are talking about a lot of drawing and planning. They wanted to catch Santa—a bold undertaking to say the very least. They plotted and planned for days, maybe even weeks. They called it "Operation Mistletoe" and gave each family member a code name so Santa would not know who they were. Dad was codenamed "Falcon" and so on. The kids planned to set up a hidden camera to catch Santa in the act. Mom and Dad would help them set up the tripod to assist them in catching St. Nick. It was all drawn out on construction paper and laid out as a family project on the dining room table for the entire month.

It was a really imaginative and complex plan. They would set the camera to start recording before bed, then check it in the morning to see their Elf on the Shelf and Santa interacting. The camera would be on a tripod in the dining room in the dark, overlooking the living room and pointed at their tree. It was flawless, right?

Mom and Dad shared the story with me, and I thought it required a bit of work from Butters the Elf and myself. We thought it was great, but it would be even better if we made a plan of our own.

We started with a video. (You can view it at emeraldlakebooks.com/mistletoe.) As Butters and Santa record regular videos, it was just one more to record in our amazing workshop. I'd be remiss if I didn't thank Rustic Country Barn in New Milford, Connecticut, for allowing us to film there over the years. Their workshop is ideal as a "Santa's Workshop" with every tool imaginable. We record many a message from this workshop, and it looks simply perfect in our proverbial toolbox of tricks and schemes.

We set the lighting a bit dark as Santa would be working late and trying to figure out this scheme that another elf had passed to him... to me. Santa was reviewing notes and called in Butters (an elf the children had met at my appearances) to consult with him on this peculiar circumstance. The video makes a solid point.

Santa will not be caught by anyone unless he chooses to be seen.

This video alerted the children that I was onto their plan. Santa, of course, sees all. I even dropped clues that I knew it was them with a wooden train of letters spelling out their family's name with blocks. They would have to search for it, but they would certainly find it.

Butters and I had a blast recording this video, including plenty of silly humor. I still laugh at the video and the memory of making it. We had *so many* re-takes because, while we were "riffing," it was making us both break down in tear-filled laughter.

At the end of the video, we made it very clear and mildly dark. Catching Santa was "naughty" and anyone trying to capture my magic risked the Naughty List. Permanently. A scary thought for anyone, but these were good kids. There was no way they'd continue.

The children received the video and watched it many times, over and over as I recall. What blew my mind was the text from their parents that said, "They want to go ahead with it." *Wow!* I was shocked. The parents decided they'd turn the camera off once the kids were in bed, put out the gifts, then turn it back on. It would show that Santa was on to them, and they'd leave a note from Santa saying, "Nope! Not gonna catch me!"

Butters and I had another idea instead. We called the parents on December 23rd and said, "Don't turn the camera off. We will come and get caught." And we did. Butters was in full costume with me (and stealing my cookies in the house). We decided to make our appearance after the kids had gone to bed on Christmas Eve. We arrived at about 2am, so the kids were woken up from a dead sleep.

The daughter came right out to see us as we were playing with the camera and eating cookies. She was thrilled to see *both* of us in person, but her brother was not to be seen. Dad came out and said, "He won't come out. He thinks he's in trouble." Well, I can't blame him. The video would have scared me too! Eventually, he snuck out of the hall shadows and proceeded to blame everyone in the family. He threw them each under the bus, saying he had no option but to go along with the story. But Santa knows the truth.

The visit ended on a wonderful note. The kids got to prove that Santa and Butters the Elf were real. We actually brought them gifts, and no one was in trouble. We took some pictures together and told them they had to go back to bed.

Operation Mistletoe will go down as one of my all-time favorite visits. It was simply hysterical and a multi-pronged approach to delivering not simply a visit, but a magic experience none of us will ever forget.

Chapter 20 – Final Chapter

WHILE THIS BOOK IS NOT long, it has taken years to put together. From my childhood experiences to the adult portrayal of Santa and finally to living as Santa. I keep my beard year 'round now. It doesn't need as much help from Sergio as it once did and remains mostly grey and white with smatterings of reddish-brown.

If it's June and I go to the store, kids whisper, "There's Santa." That can be more than I ever expected. But more times than not, I smile and engage, if only with a wink—my trademark. I go above and beyond, taking a moment of my day to make a child smile.

But why would a grown man keep a white beard when he's in his forties? I look twenty years older than I actually am. Why keep the charade all year long, and why go to such lengths to establish a company when I could just throw on a fake beard and suit to do a few appearances?

It all harkens back to the one word... the word that means everything to Santa, and truly to my soul. *Belief.*

We all need to believe in something greater than ourselves. We all need to believe in the magic of Christmas because it *is* real. We all need to believe in the love of mankind. Yeah, this sounds deep and a bit sappy, but as Santa, trust me. It's true. Santa is pure, and every adult and child knows who he is supposed to be. Not the guy who gives, but the guy who ensures you're good and then gives. Yes, Santa is a judgmental guy, but the world needs checks and balances. Children and adults know that if you're not good, you do not receive.

Maybe that's a part of it for me. I want to receive the love or confirmation of belief. That's what I get for being good as Santa. The look from adults and children alike when I am in that suit is the payoff. Seeing something pure from another person is magical.

So, when I am asked why I put in the crazy hours and make the videos and do the appearances... this book explains why. Behind the beard is a man just like any other who seeks the validation of love and light as much as the next. When I am behind the beard, I receive all of these gifts, tenfold to what I give. I have the great gift of seeing humanity at its best, if only for a short time.

And with that, I ask of you to simply share. Share this copy of the book or a new one with someone you love. (Woo-hoo, book sales!) If they feel the joy of humanity already, this will hopefully affirm their beliefs. If, however, they are lacking joy or belief in anything, my intention is that this book gives them a glimmer of light and hope that there is something greater than any individual... if they only believe.

Chapter 21 – I'll Be Back Again, Someday

I HOPE MY STORIES, TIPS AND some Santa-insight have inspired your holiday season. Remember that time is all we truly have, and it is a precious commodity. Time needs to be spent wisely, and it certainly should be spent inspiring, teaching and making children happy, while appreciating what we have and sharing that love with others. The smile of a child is where the true power lies. It inspires the sparkle in Santa's eye. It lets us all believe that mankind is going to be okay.

Children are the true gift themselves. The man in the red suit does not detract from any religious meaning or messages. Santa defines the broader message they all deliver.

Yes, as a holiday, Christmas has been over-commercialized. We all agree. We have the ability in our own homes to keep the meaning alive, though. Peace and joy are two of the greatest things to wish for in this life.

These are the broader meanings of love that most religions preach anyway, right?

For just a moment in my life, each year, I am given the greatest gift: that of personifying this joy and delivering it with a silly hat and boisterous laugh. You can deliver and feel that joy, too. You can be Santa, if you truly believe.

I must ask then... If you didn't before, do you believe now? If so, I will see you on Christmas Eve, and you will certainly see me.

May God bless your family, and may you all have a very Merry Christmas!

Thank you for reading *Behind the Beard*.
If you've enjoyed reading this book,
please leave a review on your favorite review site.
It helps me reach more parents who might enjoy
some advice from The Big Guy!

To learn how to receive a personalized video
from Santa himself to your favorite child,
visit emeraldlakebooks.com/Santavideos.

Acknowledgments

THIS BOOK WOULDN'T BE POSSIBLE without all who have supported me, visited me, written letters, requested this book be written, baked me cookies, put up with my schedule, come to see me in freezing temperatures, supported me down south, and to *all* my friends in general, who are the most amazing people. I am blessed to have you in my life. So many of you could be named, but come see me, and I'll write a personal message for you.

To those who support "Run Santa Run" and who walked with me through those days in May 2011 when I was fighting for my very life. You have stood (and sat) by my side for days, and your prayers were answered. You understand how special this is for me to be able to do.

Moreover, this book is for my family. I am proud to wear the moniker of "Buckbee" and love my family more than anything else in this world. Mom and Dad, you have made the holiday season what it is for me, and what it means to so many who visit me as Santa. They each get to feel a little bit of our family's love, which is that magic you have created in our traditions.

You have made me into the man I have become, and I cannot thank you enough for teaching me to give. The act of giving truly is the greatest gift of all.

Now, I hope we can all share that feeling of family, love and Christmas Spirit together.

Nothing Beats Family.
Thank you. I love you.
— UB

Author Bio

BILL BUCKBEE IS A COUNTRY-LIVING guy who enjoys golfing and fishing in the little free time he has. He is married to his work and is dedicated to his community.

As a full-time job, he runs the nonprofit park and museum that he grew up going to as a child. He has spent years as a youth coach of basketball, baseball and football, and has even coached semi-pro women's football. He has spent time as a volunteer firefighter and is an active Freemason.

In addition, Bill was elected as state representative in 2016 to the Connecticut General Assembly, which he highlights as the honor of a lifetime, to represent the town he loves so dearly.

Bill has spent more than 25 years playing softball and recreational league football, and his teammates are family to him.

One of three kids, Bill takes family seriously, but always with giant hugs and bigger smiles. A proud uncle to a niece and four nephews (who call him "Uncle Buck"), he can never see enough of them.

If you're interested in having Bill come speak to your group or organization, you can contact him at emeraldlakebooks.com/buckbee.

For more great books, please visit us at
emeraldlakebooks.com.

EMERALD LAKE
BOOKS

CPSIA information can be obtained
at www.ICGtesting.com
Printed in the USA
LVHW020302060820
662515LV00006B/1872